# TO KILL A MOCKINGBIRD

## Harper Lee

AUTHORED by Adam Kissel
UPDATED AND REVISED by J.N. Smith

COVER DESIGN by Table XI Partners LLC
COVER PHOTO by Olivia Verma and © 2005 GradeSaver, LLC

BOOK DESIGN by Table XI Partners LLC

Published by GradeSaver LLC, www.gradesaver.com

First published in the United States of America by GradeSaver LLC. 2009

GRADESAVER, the GradeSaver logo and the phrase "Getting you the grade since 1999" are registered trademarks of GradeSaver, LLC

ISBN 978-1-60259-174-5

Printed in the United States of America

For other products and additional information please visit
http://www.gradesaver.com

# Table of Contents

Teaching Guide - About the Author...................................................................1

Teaching Guide - Study Objectives................................................................3

Teaching Guide - Introduction to To Kill a Mockingbird........................5
    Key Aspects of To Kill a Mockingbird....................................................5
        Tone.......................................................................................................5
        Setting..................................................................................................5
        Point of View.....................................................................................5
        Character Development......................................................................5
        Themes.................................................................................................6
        Symbols................................................................................................6
        Climax..................................................................................................7
        Structure..............................................................................................7

Teaching Guide - Relationship with Other Books....................................9

Teaching Guide - Notes to the Teacher......................................................11

Day 1 - Reading Assignment..........................................................................13
    Daily Lesson Objectives.............................................................................13
    Content Summary for Teachers................................................................13
    Thought Questions (students consider while they read)....................14
    Vocabulary (in order of appearance).....................................................14
    Additional Homework.................................................................................15

Day 1 - Discussion of Thought Questions..................................................17

Day 1 - Short Answer Quiz..............................................................................21
    Short Answer Quiz Key..............................................................................23

Day 1 - Vocabulary Quiz..................................................................................25
    Vocabulary Quiz Answer Key...................................................................26

Day 1 - Classroom Activities...........................................................................27

Day 2 - Reading Assignment..........................................................................29
    Daily Lesson Objectives.............................................................................29
    Content Summary for Teachers................................................................29
    Thought Questions (students consider while they read)....................30
    Vocabulary (in order of appearance).....................................................30
    Additional Homework.................................................................................31

# Table of Contents

Day 2 - Discussion of Thought Questions..............................................33

Day 2 - Short Answer Quiz...............................................................37
    Short Answer Quiz Key.............................................................39

Day 2 - Vocabulary Quiz..................................................................41
    Vocabulary Quiz Answer Key......................................................42

Day 2 - Classroom Activities.............................................................43

Day 3 - Reading Assignment.............................................................45
    Daily Lesson Objectives.............................................................45
    Content Summary for Teachers....................................................45
    Thought Questions (students consider while they read)..........................46
    Vocabulary (in order of appearance)...............................................46
    Additional Homework................................................................48

Day 3 - Discussion of Thought Questions..............................................49

Day 3 - Short Answer Quiz...............................................................51
    Short Answer Quiz Key.............................................................53

Day 3 - Vocabulary Quiz..................................................................55
    Vocabulary Quiz Answer Key......................................................56

Day 3 - Classroom Activities.............................................................57

Day 4 - Reading Assignment.............................................................59
    Daily Lesson Objectives.............................................................59
    Content Summary for Teachers....................................................59
    Thought Questions (students consider while they read)..........................61
    Vocabulary (in order of appearance)...............................................61
    Additional Homework................................................................62

Day 4 - Discussion of Thought Questions..............................................63

Day 4 - Short Answer Quiz...............................................................67
    Short Answer Quiz Key.............................................................69

Day 4 - Vocabulary Quiz..................................................................71
    Vocabulary Quiz Answer Key......................................................72

# Table of Contents

Day 4 - Classroom Activities..................................................................73

Day 5 - Reading Assignment.................................................................75
    Daily Lesson Objectives.................................................................75
    Content Summary for Teachers.......................................................75
    Thought Questions (students consider while they read).............77
    Vocabulary (in order of appearance)...............................................77
    Additional Homework.....................................................................78

Day 5 - Discussion of Thought Questions........................................79

Day 5 - Short Answer Quiz.................................................................83
    Short Answer Quiz Key...................................................................85

Day 5 - Vocabulary Quiz.....................................................................87
    Vocabulary Quiz Answer Key.........................................................88

Day 5 - Classroom Activities..............................................................89

Final Paper...........................................................................................91
    Essay Questions.............................................................................91
    Advice on research sources.............................................................91
    Grading rubric for essays...............................................................92
    Final Paper Answer Key.................................................................93

Final Exam...........................................................................................97
    A. Multiple Choice........................................................................97
    B. Short Answer...........................................................................100
    C. Vocabulary..............................................................................101
    D. Short Essays...........................................................................102

Final Exam Answer Key....................................................................105
    A. Multiple Choice Answer Key...................................................105
    B. Short Answer Key....................................................................105
    C. Vocabulary Answer Key...........................................................105
    D. Short Essays Answer Key.........................................................106

# Teaching Guide - About the Author

**Harper Lee** is known best as the author of *To Kill a Mockingbird*. She was born on April 28, 1926, in a small southwestern Alabama town named Monroeville. Her novel also takes place in Alabama and is told by a female narrator. Lee never published a second novel, perhaps because *To Kill a Mockingbird* set such a high standard. Or perhaps her life illustrates the maxim that everyone could find something in his or her life experience that could become a novel; everyone has one novel inside.

As a child, Lee was a tomboy and a precocious reader, and she enjoyed the friendship of her schoolmate and neighbor, the young Truman Capote, another American author. They worked together on writing projects and remained friends. Capote in some ways became the character of Dill in *To Kill a Mockingbird*, and the narrator, Scout, could be a version of the young Harper Lee.

When Lee was five years old, Alabama was rocked by the trials of nine black men for the alleged rape of two white women. Although most if not all of the men were innocent, an all-white jury sentenced most of them to death. Over the following years, the story stayed in the news as the convictions were reversed, and this story became a source for the novel.

Lee was 34 years old in 1960, when she published the novel.

# Teaching Guide - Study Objectives

If all of the elements of this lesson plan are employed, students will develop the following powers, skills, and understanding:

1. Reading well: appreciating the achievement of the author by examining and discussing details and overarching themes and considering how the details contribute to the whole novel; enjoying a good book in the company of other readers.

2. Thinking well: using the discussion questions to draw conclusions from evidence and to use evidence to weigh arguments and counterarguments.

3. Speaking well: developing oral skills through vocabulary development, debate, dramatic readings, and group discussion.

4. Listening well: developing a taste for good grammar and strong diction; evaluating oral arguments.

5. Writing well: creating and sustaining an argument, using evidence, in essay form.

6. Understanding: seeing how themes of growing up, race, gender, class, and family play out in a scenario that remains relevant to students today.

# Teaching Guide - Introduction to To Kill a Mockingbird

When Harper Lee wrote *To Kill a Mockingbird*, race relations in the South, particularly in Alabama, were poor. The South was still segregated, forcing blacks and white to use different facilities in almost every aspect of society. The Civil Rights Movement began to pick up steam when Rosa Parks refused to give up her seat on a bus in Montgomery, Alabama, in 1955. Issues of race were receiving serious national attention, and the time was perfect for a novel such as To Kill a Mockingbird, which examines the injustice of racism and inequality in the American South. The novel is set in the 1930s in Alabama.

The novel is also about how a young girl grows up and learns her way in a specific cultural setting. Scout Finch works to come to terms with the existence of social and racial inequality in her society. She also, for a while, resents the efforts of adults to make her into a "proper Southern lady."

## Key Aspects of To Kill a Mockingbird

### Tone

Note that the tone is different at different points in the book. Some examples of tone or the settings that produce tone: the hot, lazy days of summer; fear of the Radley house; being young and unencumbered; racial tension in the courtroom, at the jail, and at Calpurnia's church; adults putting on airs; Atticus's even keel; the hilarious tone of the pageant; the suspenseful fight at the end.

### Setting

Maycomb County, Alabama, early 1930s

### Point of View

First-person narration, the recollection of Jean Louise (Scout) Finch

### Character Development

Jem and Scout grow up from childhood to early adolescence; they are socialized into the gendered roles of young adults. Atticus develops his understanding that sometimes a lie is the best thing (recall that he already would look the other way when Mr. Ewell would hunt out of season). Arthur Radley turns out to be less scary and more compassionate than the children think, but he is still capable of killing Mr. Ewell. Aunt Alexandra does not really budge in her ideas of who the Fine Folks are and what it means to be a lady and an upstanding citizen. Tom Robinson loses hope. Mr. Ewell gets even more angry after being shamed in the courtroom.

## Themes

small-town life; racism; class differences; growing up; parenting and role models; justice; honesty vs. hypocrisy; loss of innocence; gossip

- **Justice**: Atticus, father of Scout and Jem, is a moral teacher for his children as well as for the town. When Atticus speaks, it is worth considering what principles of justice he is promoting. One also can track Scout's maturation as she develops her own ideas about justice. Finally, one can examine how principles of justice guide law enforcement, moral standards in the town, and the trial.

- **Education**: As Jem and Scout grow up, they are educated by watching and listening in the town and by the adults around them, not just by formal schooling. The children also learn from one another and from their experience. Thus, each episode involving them can be considered from the perspective of what the children might learn, or do learn, from the episode.

- **Social Inequality**: Since age, race, class, and gender differences are fundamental to this novel, readers can analyze many scenes by examining any inequalities they note, such as where and how people live or how different people act, speak, dress, and are treated by others. A teacher can help students think not only about group differences but also about how individual differences such as temperament make each person distinct.

- **Mockingbird**: Tracking a specific symbol depends on identifying the places it appears in the novel and elaborating on the function of the symbol in each context.

## Symbols

Mockingbird: innocence and kindness; Tom Robinson

Blue jay: rapaciousness and injustice; Robert Ewell

Radley house: the unknown; evil

Ham: comedy; Maycomb County

# Climax

The initial climax of the Tom Robinson story occurs as the verdict is being read, although the point of most energy occurs during Mayella's cross-examination. There is a second, more proper climax in this story as Robert Ewell attacks the children and is killed. That scene is also the climax of the Arthur Radley story; Boo Radley's character is summed up in the moment when he kills Ewell and saves the children.

# Structure

There are several overlapping tales in this book. One involves Boo Radley and the Radley house from the perspective of the children (including Dill); they play all summer and consider the Radley house a taboo they break by enacting dramas about it. During the school year, they continue to avoid the house. The second tale involves the Ewells and Robinsons and Atticus Finch's defense of Mr. Robinson. These two main tales do not come together until the final climax of the novel.

Structure

# Teaching Guide - Relationship with Other Books

## Ways to discuss other books

Consider other books that are told from the perspective of a child, such as *The Catcher in the Rye* and *A Portrait of the Artist as a Young Man*.

Consider other books that treat racism, such as *Uncle Tom's Cabin*.

Consider other works that involve a court case, such as *Inherit the Wind* and *The Crucible*.

## How to employ a Socratic method when teaching this book (or how to engage students in discussion of this book)

Students will be able to provide stories from their own childhoods about people or buildings that they feared. From there, engage students in tales of how they have been socialized towards becoming an adult and specifically a man or a woman.

Using this book to launch a full-scale discussion of race and racism will distract students from the goals of an AP English course, but many students will be able to use this theme as an entrée to the novel.

The court case will attract students naturally. Use this interest to encourage a close reading of the lawyers' strategies for examining a witness. Likewise, use interest in the drama of the final fight to produce a close reading of the facts.

# Teaching Guide - Notes to the Teacher

The thought questions in this lesson plan provide material and ideas that students can use to write short original essays. For the sake of improving the power of expression, teachers should encourage students to write on topics that have been discussed in class, this time in the more formal writing style expected in a literary essay. At the same time, students should not be discouraged from choosing their own topics.

The questions provided for the final paper are most suitable for student essays. Remember that grading an essay should not depend on a simple checklist of required content.

# Day 1 - Reading Assignment

Students read chapters 1-6.

## Daily Lesson Objectives

- Introduction to reading well: learning how to get acquainted with a new work of literature by examining characters, tone, and setting; finding early themes; appreciating the achievement of good writing.
- Introduction to thinking well: using the discussion questions to do more than just read.
- Introduction to speaking well: developing oral skills through vocabulary development and discussion of thought questions.

Note that it is perfectly fine to expand any day's work into two days depending on the characteristics of the class, particularly if the class will engage in all of the suggested classroom exercises and activities and discuss all of the thought questions.

## Content Summary for Teachers

**Chapter 1**: Introduction to the Finch family, the Radley family, and Depression-era Maycomb. Scout's and Jem's mother died of a heart attack when Scout was two. Now Scout is almost six, and Jem is almost ten. Their feisty friend Dill is almost seven. It is summer. Boo Radley is locked inside and is cared for by his older brother Nathan. The children are intrigued about Boo Radley, and Jem screws up the courage to touch the house.

**Chapter 2**: The summer is over, and it is September. Scout is in school, and Miss Caroline is trying to enforce a specific way of learning to read and write. Scout explains the poverty of the Cunninghams.

**Chapter 3**: Jem has Walter Cunningham over for lunch. Back at school, Miss Caroline is having a hard time as a new teacher. Scout feels discouraged about school, but Atticus persuades her to keep trying. Atticus adds that the town bends the law for the Ewells because they will never change their ways and they are so poor they need to hunt out of season.

**Chapter 4**: School continues. In front of Radley house, someone seems to be leaving gifts for the children in the knothole of an oak tree. In the summer, Dill returns. They roll a tire by mistake into the Radleys' yard. The children create a complex dramatic reenactment of all the gossip they have heard about Boo and his family. After Atticus catches them doing a reenactment, they stop.

**Chapter 5**: Jem and Dill have become closer friends, and Scout, being a girl, is often excluded from their play. Scout often sits with their neighbor, Maudie Atkinson.

They discuss Boo. Jem and Dill try to leave a note for Boo using a fishing line, asking him to come out, but Atticus catches them.

**Chapter 6**: On the last night of summer for Dill, the children sneak over to Boo's house. They see a shadow, get scared, and run away, with Jem losing his pants in the gate. There is a gunshot, and the neighbors gather. Mr. Radley says he was shooting at a "white Negro" in his back yard. Dill makes up a story about playing strip poker to explain Jem's missing pants. Jem goes back for his pants and returns with them, trembling.

# Thought Questions (students consider while they read)

1. What does it mean that "You never really understand a person … until you climb into his skin and walk around in it" (ch. 3)?
2. Why does Atticus Finch say that Bob Ewell should be allowed to break the law by "hunting out of season" (ch. 3)?
3. What do you think about what Jem calls the "Dewey Decimal System" of education (ch. 2 and ch. 4)? How is it a valuable or a poor system?
4. What does Miss Maudie mean when she says, "That is three-fourths colored folks and one-fourth Stephanie Crawford" (ch. 5)? What are some other ideas that white characters express about black characters or about other white characters?
5. What does it take to be the kind of person who "is the same in his house as he is on the public streets" (ch. 5)?
6. What does it mean that "What Mr. Radley did might seem peculiar to us, but it did not seem peculiar to him"(ch. 5)? Is he peculiar or not?

# Vocabulary (in order of appearance)

**Chapter 1**:

- assuaged: soothed; lessened the pain
- maintain (as in "posit"): posit, assert
- chattels: items owned
- trot-lines: cords with multiple fishing hooks
- unsullied: not dirty
- imprudent: not prudent, not wise or practical
- tyrannical: like a tyrant, like an authoritarian
- transition: a change

**Chapter 2**:

- condescended: looked down on from a position of real or imagined authority

- misfortunes: experiences with negative outcomes
- crimson: the red color of blood
- indigenous: characterized by being local
- entailment: a condition on owning property
- smilax: a kind of flowering plant
- vexations: troublesome situations
- sojourn: to stay somewhere for a short time

## Chapter 3:

- dispensation: a giving-out or distribution, an abstract gift
- haint: ghost
- iniquities: sins
- phenomenal: really wonderful
- contemptuous: with contempt, with disdain
- diminutive: quite small
- misdemeanor: a minor crime
- concessions: acknowledgments in favor of the other side in an argument
- disapprobation: disapproval

## Chapter 4:

- auspicious: suggesting good luck
- scuppernongs: sweet grapes
- evasion: avoidance

## Chapter 5:

- benign: not problematic
- chameleon: lizard-like animal that can change color to match its background, or a person who flip-flops based on the context
- benevolence: goodwill
- morbid: on the theme of death
- incomprehensible: not understandable
- inquisitive: curious
- dryly: without much emotion and almost sarcastic

## Chapter 6:

- malignant: hurtful or even deadly
- desolate: deserted, ruined

# Additional Homework

1. Learn something about John Dewey's views of childhood education. Write up to one paragraph about these views.

2. Make sure you can locate Alabama on a map of the United States.

Additional Homework

# Day 1 - Discussion of Thought Questions

1. What does it mean that "You never really understand a person ... until you climb into his skin and walk around in it" (ch. 3)?

   **Time**: 5 minutes

   **Discussion**: Understanding someone means seeing the world from his or her point of view. (See activity below.) It also means imagining what someone's views would be if he or she had certain experiences. Consider how Jean Louise understands the Cunninghams and describes them to her new teacher, who is from out of town.

2. Why does Atticus Finch say that Bob Ewell should be allowed to break the law by "hunting out of season" (ch. 3)?

   **Time**: 5 minutes

   **Discussion**:

   Atticus says that common people should obey the law, but people like the Ewells need special treatment. They break the law so often that it takes more of society's resources to charge them than it does to leave them alone and suffer the consequences. They don't go to school, and Mr. Ewell hunts and traps out of season, but putting him in jail will only hurt his family and will not rehabilitate Mr. Ewell. Out of compassion for his family, we look the other way after their crimes.

   Note that the failure to rehabilitate Mr. Ewell actually will cause great costs to society in the future (but do not reveal the ending).

3. What do you think about what Jem calls the "Dewey Decimal System" of education (ch. 2 and ch. 4)? How is it a valuable or a poor system?

   **Time**: 5 minutes

**Discussion**: The system seems to assume that students in each grade have a certain educational level, but the children in Maycomb are not necessarily at that level. Jean Louise is way ahead in reading, and it seems that the system is not flexible enough to teach her at her actual reading level. When Miss Caroline complains about Jean Louise reading at home, it is unclear whether this is a rule in the "system" or if it is just Miss Caroline's idea. But when she complains about Jean Louise writing in cursive, she says, "we don't write in the first grade, we print. You won't learn to write until you're in the third grade."

4. What does Miss Maudie mean when she says, "That is three-fourths colored folks and one-fourth Stephanie Crawford" (ch. 5)? What are some other ideas that white characters express about black characters or about other white characters?

**Time**: 5-10 minutes

**Discussion**: Miss Maudie means that there is a lot of gossip and speculation in Maycomb. She suggests that a lot of it comes from black citizens, but a lot also comes from Stephanie Crawford. In a small community, it seems that everyone knows everyone else's business (consider gossip at your school and how often it is true or false). In chapter 2, white citizens clearly have separated themselves by class; consider what Jean Louise says about the Cunninghams, and Atticus says that Mr. Cunningham "came from a set breed of men." In chapter 3, Atticus points out that it is not only poor citizens who have a hard time getting an education in Maycomb, but also the black citizens, when he says that Calpurnia has "more education than most colored folks." He also says that the Ewells have been "the disgrace of Maycomb for three generations," partly because they do not work for a living, but also because "they lived like animals."

5. What does it take to be the kind of person who "is the same in his house as he is on the public streets" (ch. 5)?

**Time**: 5 minutes

**Discussion**: According to Miss Maudie, Atticus does not show hypocrisy. He is the same in private as he is in public. Whatever principles of honor and conduct he talks about on the street, he tries to live out at home. It takes a strong sense of honesty and good character to be that way. Just because nobody sees you in private, it does not mean you are free from doing what is right.

6. What does it mean that "What Mr. Radley did might seem peculiar to us, but it did not seem peculiar to him"(ch. 5)? Is he peculiar or not?

**Time**: 5 minutes

**Discussion**: The question here is whether there are natural standards of decency and normality for human beings, and if they are, what are they? People shouldn't "live like animals" like the Ewells, but what does it mean to live like humans? It is not normal to spend one's whole life indoors, and it is not usually healthy. But shouldn't we make exceptions for people in special cases? Clearly some things in human life are not subject to the judgment of others, such as what kind of exercise people like to do, but some things are essential for a human being to meet his or her full potential.

# Day 1 - Short Answer Quiz

1. Name the three members of the Finch family.

_____

2. Name the Finch's housekeeper.

_____

3. What is the name of the Finch children's best friend?

_____

4. In what state does the novel take place?

_____

5. Who loses his pants at Boo Radley's house?

_____

6. Who is the protagonist in the story?

_____

7. Who, so far, seems to be the antagonist in the story?

_____

8. Is the setting of the story a big city, a small town, or a farming community?

_____

9. Which term best describes the plot of chapters 1-6? Rising action, falling action, or climax?

_____

10. Who is the narrator?

_____

11. Choose one of the Finch children and use two adjectives to describe him or her.

_____

12. What do you find most interesting about these chapters?

_____

# Short Answer Quiz Key

1. Atticus, Jem, Jean Louise (a.k.a. Scout)
2. Calpurnia
3. Dill
4. Alabama
5. Jem Finch
6. Jean Louise Finch
7. Boo Radley [Arthur Radley]. (See activity below.)
8. a small town
9. rising action
10. Jean Louise Finch
11. many possible answers
12. many possible answers

# Day 1 - Vocabulary Quiz

### Terms

1. _____ assuaged
2. _____ auspicious
3. _____ benevolence
4. _____ benign
5. _____ concession
6. _____ condescended
7. _____ contemptuous
8. _____ desolate
9. _____ diminutive
10. _____ dryly
11. _____ evasion
12. _____ imprudent
13. _____ malignant
14. _____ misdemeanor
15. _____ morbid
16. _____ sojourn
17. _____ transition
18. _____ tyrannical
19. _____ unsullied
20. _____ vexations

### Answers

A. quite small
B. avoidance
C. like an authoritarian
D. soothed; lessened the pain
E. hurtful or even deadly
F. acknowledgment in favor of the other side in an argument
G. suggesting good luck
H. not wise or practical
I. a minor crime
J. goodwill
K. with disdain
L. on the theme of death
M. deserted, ruined
N. a change
O. not problematic
P. not dirty
Q. without much emotion
R. to stay somewhere for a short time
S. looked down on from a position of real or imagined authority
T. troublesome situations

# Vocabulary Quiz Answer Key

1. D
2. G
3. J
4. O
5. F
6. S
7. K
8. M
9. A
10. Q
11. B
12. H
13. E
14. I
15. L
16. R
17. N
18. C
19. P
20. T

# Day 1 - Classroom Activities

1. Why was race so important when the novel was published?

**Kind of Activity**: whole class
**Objective**: to understand the historical context of the novel's publication
**Time**: 10-15 minutes

**Structure**: *To Kill a Mockingbird* was published in 1960 as the Civil Rights Movement was growing in the United States. Racial segregation was a significant social problem in Alabama and throughout the southern United States. Help students gain a sense of the power of racism at that time by means of images, text, audio, and video from the 1950s and 1960s from the Civil Rights Movement. History teachers at your school might already have good materials on the subject. Consider using video of civil rights marches and rallies that involve police brutality or of the federal government enforcing desegregation, video or audio excerpts from Martin Luther King's speeches, period poetry, and excerpts from the Civil Rights Act of 1964 and the U.S. Constitution and Declaration of Independence regarding human equality and nondiscrimination. Also consider retelling the story of the black Alabama men who were wrongly convicted of rape (see "About the Author"). This context should not distract students from focusing on the novel itself, but teachers should remember that these events of half a century ago might seem quite foreign to most students.

2. Who is an "outsider"? What is an antagonist?

**Kind of Activity**: small group activity
**Objective**: to consider why some people are labeled as "outsiders" by others
**Time**: 15-20 minutes

**Structure**:

Ask the question, Who are the antagonists, and why do people feel antagonistic toward them? Each small group is assigned one of the following for five minutes (simultaneously) and then reports to the class for two minutes (severally):

* Boo Radley (seems scary; has a violent past)

* Mrs. Dubose (mean)

* The Ewells (poor and a "disgrace")

* Miss Caroline Fisher (the teacher with alternative ideas about education)

* Blacks (to some of the white characters)

**Assessment Criteria**:

* students demonstrate knowledge of the character

* use of evidence from the text

* speaking skills

3. Dill's Summer Theater

**Kind of Activity**: small groups performing for the class
**Objective**: to practice playful improvisation
**Time**: 15-20 minutes

**Structure**:

In chapter 1, Dill is a great storyteller. All summer, Dill and the other children make up dramas that they act out for fun. Divide the class into three or four groups and give them three or four minutes to choose a story they will act out and to assign roles. They should select well-known stories from popular culture or other readings they have shared. Not every person in the group needs a role. After that, the students start to improvise the stories they have selected. The point of this exercise is to let students experience the fun of storytelling as they retell a story to one another in character.

Afterward, introduce the concept of a "play within a play" (there are stories and fictions within the novel itself) and note that Harper Lee is focusing on storytelling in part because she herself is a storyteller. How can we distinguish a true story from one that is being made up for fun?

**Assessment Criteria**:

* students are participating, paying attention, and enjoying themselves

* speaking skills

* creativity

# Day 2 - Reading Assignment

Students read chapters 7-11.

## Daily Lesson Objectives

- Work on reading well: learning how to track themes and characters; appreciating the narrative structure of achievement of good writing.
- Introduction to thinking well: using the discussion questions to do more than just read; assessing the oral reading of peers.
- Introduction to speaking well: developing oral skills through vocabulary development, discussion of thought questions, and reading aloud.
- Expressive skill: drawing caricatures.
- Understanding race: considering how the town reacts as Atticus, a white lawyer, defends a black man against serious legal charges.
- Introduction to justice and courage: considering why it is "a sin" to kill a mockingbird, why Atticus defends Robinson, and why Jem must read to Mrs. Dubose after cutting up her flowers.

Note that it is perfectly fine to expand any day's work into two days depending on the characteristics of the class, particularly if the class will engage in all of the suggested classroom exercises and activities and discuss all of the thought questions.

## Content Summary for Teachers

**Chapter 7**: In the new school year, Scout is bored in the second grade. Jem reveals that he found his lost pants all folded up. Jem and Scout find a ball of twine, soap figures, and more gifts in the knothole of the Radley oak tree. They leave a note of thanks in the tree but find, the next day, that someone filled the hole with cement.

**Chapter 8**: It is winter. Mrs. Radley dies. School is canceled because of snow. Jem and Scout make a snowman with soil and snow; the snowman looks like a distorted Mr. Avery. Atticus persuades them to disguise the snowman, so they make it look like Miss Maudie. The next night, Miss Maudie's house catches on fire. The children watch and shiver in the cold. Boo Radley mysteriously wraps a blanket around Scout's shoulders without her knowledge.

**Chapter 9**: Scout learns that people are talking because her father has agreed to defend a black man, Tom Robinson, from legal charges. Atticus notes that defending Robinson is a matter of personal honor and justice. Atticus persuades Scout to hold her head up, not to fight, and to respect others in the town even if they disapprove. Over at Finch's Landing, Aunt Alexandra presses Scout to be ladylike, but Scout punches Francis when he criticizes Atticus for defending Robinson. Uncle Jack and Atticus discuss the issue, and Atticus acknowledges that the criticism around town will continue. It will be the word of a white family against a black man. Atticus lets

Scout overhear the conversation.

**Chapter 10**: Scout is slightly ashamed of her bookish father. Atticus tells Scout and Jem they can shoot at tins cans and bluebirds, but it is a sin to kill a mockingbird. Mockingbirds make music and do not make any trouble. A rabid dog appears in the neighborhood, and Atticus reluctantly but accurately shoots it. A gun seems like an unfair advantage over other living beings. Jem believes Atticus is a gentleman.

**Chapter 11**: Mrs. Dubose is mean, old, and sick. She yells at Jem and Scout. One day she yells about how Atticus is no better than "the [black] trash he works for." Atticus discusses standing up for justice and conscience regardless of what others think. Jem and Scout go into town, and Scout buys a baton. On their way home, Jem suddenly and angrily cuts off the tops of Mrs. Dubose's camellia bushes and then snaps the baton in half. Atticus makes Jem apologize to Mrs. Dubose in person. Jem also must read to Mrs. Dubose every afternoon for a month. She listens and complains each day. At the end of the month, she asks for one more week. Weeks later, she dies, but Jem's reading helped her die with courage and dignity, free of the morphine painkillers.

# Thought Questions (students consider while they read)

1. What are the children learning in school? How else are they learning about themselves and their society? (ch. 7)
2. How are the children in the novel creative? (ch. 8)
3. How is Boo Radley showing compassion for the children? (ch. 7 and ch. 8)
4. Why is Atticus Finch defending Tom Robinson? (ch. 9)
5. Why is it "a sin to kill a mockingbird" (ch. 10)?

# Vocabulary (in order of appearance)

**Chapter 7**:

- embalm: to keep tissue from decomposing with a preservation process
- tarnished: sullied

**Chapter 8**:

- unfathomable: not understandable
- Rosetta Stone: an ancient stone with the same words in three different languages, which became a key to translation
- aberrations: slight disorders or problems
- Appomattox: the location of the battle that ended the U.S. Civil War
- switch (as in "peachtree switches"): slender stick used as a whip
- libel: publication of false material that ruins someone's reputation

- caricatures: distorted images
- perplexity: confusion

**Chapter 9**:

- gastric: pertaining to the stomach
- Missouri Compromise: an agreement between pro-slavery and anti-slavery politicians which permitted slavery in some areas (Missouri and Arkansas) and prohibited it in others (areas northwest)
- Stonewall Jackson (Old Blue Light): a confederate general during the Civil War. "Stonewall" refers to a comment made by General Barnard Bee in 1861: "Yonder stands Jackson like a stone wall; let's go to his assistance. Rally behind the Virginians!" "Old Blue Light" refers to Jackson in a famous poem and song from 1862, "Stonewall Jackson's Way."
- lineaments: distinctive features or shapes
- ingenuous: sincere
- diversions: distractions
- analogous: similar
- gallantly: gentlemanly
- House of Commons: the lower house of Parliament in Britain, similar to the U.S. House of Representatives

**Chapter 10**:

- attributes: characteristics
- inconspicuous: hard to notice
- mausoleum: an above-ground tomb, often large enough for visitors

**Chapter 11**:

- melancholy: sad
- reconnaissance: intelligence-gathering
- undulate: vibrate with ups and downs like a wave
- cantankerous: contentious, prone to grumble

# Additional Homework

1. What was Alabama's role in the Civil War?

Students should read one or two summaries of Alabama's role in the Civil War online (e.g., at Wikipedia: http://en.wikipedia.org/wiki/Alabama_in_the_American_Civil_War). Then, they can write up to one paragraph about the most interesting thing they learned. Some students will choose to write about the role of slaves. Thousands of slaves were forced to help the South in the war, and thousands of them escaped and joined the North. Other students might note that there were many white Unionists in Alabama who did not want to fight either. Others might note the proportion of soldiers who died of disease (about 15 percent).

# Day 2 - Discussion of Thought Questions

1. What are the children learning in school? How else are they learning about themselves and their society? (ch. 7)

**Time**: 10 minutes

**Discussion**:

The first grade class seems to have a lot of laughter but no learning. The second grade still uses the "Dewey" system and is not matched to Jean Louise's level. Jem learns about Egypt and decides to emulate what he sees on hieroglyphics. But the children are learning more outside of school from their father and Calpurnia.

They also are learning the ways of ladies and gentlemen in Maycomb by observing and emulating others. In chapter 9, Uncle Jack insists that Jean Louise wants "to grow up to be a lady," although she disagrees and likes to wear overalls instead of dresses. Aunt Alexandra feels the way Uncle Jack does, but Atticus is not in any rush to socialize his daughter. Note the symbol: "You'll have a very unladylike scar on your wedding-ring finger."

As for Jem, Jean Louise already knows that "Boys don't cook." But Jem is too young to learn the virtues of a real gentleman; what impresses him most is Atticus's skill in shooting a gun. At the end of chapter 10, he decides, "Atticus is a gentleman, just like me!" Being able to pull the trigger bravely, when necessary, is a virtue, but Atticus prefers to teach other virtues to his son.

2. How are the children in the novel creative? (ch. 8)

**Time**: 5 minutes

**Discussion**: They create a snowman made mostly out of things other than snow. They decide to make the snowman look like Mr. Avery. Consider also the great dramas that Jem and Jean Louise design and perform with Dill, and consider Dill's fanciful stories. Is creativity something you can learn in school? Does practice make us more creative?

3. How is Boo Radley showing compassion for the children? (ch. 7 and ch. 8)

**Time**: 5 minutes

**Discussion**: Boo (we think) folded up Jem's pants after he lost them at Boo's house. Boo (most likely) gives them gifts in the tree. He also probably is the one who puts a blanket on Jean Louise during the fire at Miss Maudie's house. So, is Boo the bad and scary man in the children's nightmares? Or is Harper Lee foreshadowing other good things that Boo Radley will do?

4. Why is Atticus Finch defending Tom Robinson? (ch. 9)

**Time**: 10 minutes

**Discussion**: "For a number of reasons," Atticus says. For one, it is a matter of respect for the law. He was assigned the case and has a duty to defend the man. Also, people are considered equal before the law, and it is a matter of honor to uphold the law and his country's system of government. And this case "affects him personally." (Why?) Atticus also sees that the whole town's way of life, with regard to racism, is tied up in this case. He will defend Tom Robinson even if most other people in the town do not respect him for it. He knows the task "couldn't be worse" (chapter 9), because it is a black man's word against a white man's, and Maycomb is a racist county, but Atticus says, "Before I'm through, I intend to jar the jury a bit," to help them see something about the injustice of their racism. In chapter 11, he says that it is a matter of conscience in doing the right thing, for himself and before God. If Mrs. Dubose is "the bravest person I ever knew" (ch. 11), it is because she acted in the way she thought was right, despite the extreme pain of her disease, and "she died beholden to nothing and nobody."

5. Why is it "a sin to kill a mockingbird" (ch. 10)?

**Time**: 5 minutes

**Discussion**: Blue jays eat out of people's gardens, but mockingbirds "make music for us to enjoy." The mockingbird will be a symbol for other innocent people who try to do good things (such as Tom Robinson and Arthur Radley). The rabid dog has done nothing wrong, and Atticus resists shooting it, but the dog is likely to cause serious harm in the near future. The dog might be a symbol of the rabid Mr. Ewell, who is killed near the end of the novel.

# Day 2 - Short Answer Quiz

1. Which animal does Atticus shoot?

_____

2. Who suffers from a fire in her house?

_____

3. Whom does Jean Louise fight with at Christmas?

_____

4. What drug was Mrs. Dubose addicted to?

_____

5. Who has to read *Ivanhoe* to Mrs. Dubose?

_____

6. Which figure of speech is involved when Jean remembers that Mrs. Dubose's mouth moved "out and in, like a clam hole at low tide"?

_____

7. What genre is *To Kill a Mockingbird*: poetry, drama, or prose?

_____

8. Use two adjectives to describe Mrs. Dubose.

_____

9. Is Jean Louise a reliable narrator? Why or why not?

_____

# Short Answer Quiz Key

1. a dog
2. Miss Maudie
3. Francis
4. morphine
5. Jem Finch
6. simile
7. prose
8. The many possible answers include old, sick, mean, angry, addicted, dying, and more.
9. She is not very reliable, because she is reflecting on her memories as a young girl. At the same time, it is not clear that she is wrong about what she remembers. The point of this question is to generate thought about the topic, so any reasonable and tho

# Day 2 - Vocabulary Quiz

### Terms

1. _____ aberrations
2. _____ analogous
3. _____ Appomattox
4. _____ attributes
5. _____ cantankerous
6. _____ caricatures
7. _____ diversions
8. _____ embalm
9. _____ gastric
10. _____ inconspicuous
11. _____ ingenuous
12. _____ libel
13. _____ mausoleum
14. _____ perplexity
15. _____ reconnaissance
16. _____ Rosetta Stone
17. _____ switch
18. _____ tarnished
19. _____ undulate
20. _____ unfathomable

### Answers

A. vibrate up and down like a wave
B. pertaining to the stomach
C. intelligence-gathering
D. characteristics
E. hard to notice
F. confusion
G. distorted images
H. above-ground tomb
I. battle that ended the U.S. Civil War
J. distractions
K. slight disorders or problems
L. to keep tissue from decomposing with a preservation process
M. contentious, prone to grumble
N. publication of false material that ruins someone's reputation
O. not understandable
P. sincere
Q. slender stick used as a whip
R. similar
S. sullied
T. famous translation tablet

# Vocabulary Quiz Answer Key

1. K
2. R
3. I
4. D
5. M
6. G
7. J
8. L
9. B
10. E
11. P
12. N
13. H
14. F
15. C
16. T
17. Q
18. S
19. A
20. O

# Day 2 - Classroom Activities

1. Caricature drawing

   **Kind of Activity**: individual activity
   **Objective**: to develop creativity in satire
   **Time**: 10-15 minutes

   **Structure**:

   When the snow falls, the children do not just make a snowman; they make it as a caricature of a character in the novel. A caricature or satire emphasizes key recognizable features of someone. Some caricatures just make fun of others, but some caricatures emphasize features in order to make a serious point. Choose someone famous or a character from the novel and draw a caricature of that person.

   If a caricature is particularly good, consider making a transparency of it for the next class to see if the class can guess who it is. Point out the features that make it good.

   **Assessment Criteria**:

   * students demonstrate knowledge of the person

   * creativity

   * expressive skills

2. Reading aloud

   **Kind of Activity**: whole class
   **Objective**: to practice reading aloud to an audience
   **Time**: 10 minutes

   **Structure**: Jem's punishment is to read aloud to Mrs. Dubose for a month. Reading aloud for an audience requires voice expression and pacing so that the audience can understand and appreciate what is being said. Choose several paragraphs from the readings and ask students, in turn, to read aloud a paragraph at a time. Encourage the students to consider how easy it is to understand and appreciate the text based on the expression, tone of voice, speed, and other attributes of the reading.

**Assessment Criteria**:

\* speaking skills

\* critical listening skills

# Day 3 - Reading Assignment

Students read chapters 12–17.

## Daily Lesson Objectives

- Reading well: continuing to track themes; examining character development (especially as the children age and as readers learn more about Atticus); appreciating how the author constructs the courtroom scene.
- Thinking well: using the discussion questions to draw conclusions from evidence and to use evidence to weigh arguments and counterarguments, particularly as students consider the testimony at the trial.
- Speaking well: developing oral skills through vocabulary development, debate, dramatic readings, and group discussion.
- Listening well: assessing the dramatic reading; developing a taste for good grammar and strong diction; evaluating oral arguments; paying attention to the reactions of one's peers in the "jellybean" exercise.
- Understanding: seeing how themes of socialization and exclusion play out in a social group.

Note that it is perfectly fine to expand any day's work into two days depending on the characteristics of the class, particularly if the class will engage in all of the suggested classroom exercises and activities and discuss all of the thought questions.

## Content Summary for Teachers

**Chapter 12**: Atticus leaves for two weeks for an emergency session in the state legislature. Calpurnia takes the children to her all-black church. At the church, a black woman is inhospitable to the white children, but the rest of the congregation is welcoming. The reverend exhorts the congregation to raise ten dollars for Robinson's wife and children. Scout learns that Robinson is in jail on the charge of raping Bob Ewell's daughter. As Calpurnia, Jem, and Scout arrive home, they find Aunt Alexandra sitting on their porch.

**Chapter 13**: Aunt Alexandra, old-fashioned and proper, starts educating the children with traditional habits and values. She also pressures Atticus into telling the children why they should behave and "live up to your name." Atticus tries, but after Scout begins to get upset with this strange new side of her father, he returns to his original principles and patterns.

**Chapter 14**: Scout learns what rape is. Aunt Alexandra is unhappy about the visit to Calpurnia's church and tries to make Atticus fire Calpurnia, but he refuses because Calpurnia has been so good in the family. Dill turns up, having run away from home. Jim, now feeling mature, decides that Atticus must be told. Dill stays the night.

**Chapter 15**: Dill stays for the summer. The impending trial takes its toll on the town and on Atticus. A group of men accost Atticus at home on a Saturday. Robinson is to be moved to the Maycomb jail on Sunday for the trial on Monday. They warn Atticus that others might cause trouble at the jail. Atticus holds watch at the jail on Sunday night, and his children secretly follow. A group of angry men arrives. Just as a confrontation is about to start, Scout and Jem come out of hiding. The men are determined. Scout sees Mr. Cunningham among them and innocently engages him in conversation. The men are suddenly somehow humanized, and they leave.

**Chapter 16**: Back at home, Atticus explains that some people can forget that they are human beings when they become part of a mob. The trial begins, and the children go to watch. Outside the courthouse, they chat with Mr. Raymond, who pretends he is an alcoholic, a white man who married and had children with a black woman. The courthouse is packed, and the sit up in the balcony with the black townspeople. The judge seems good and sensible.

**Chapter 17**: The trial begins. Heck Tate testifies. Mr. Ewell brought him after claiming that Mayella had been raped. He says he found Mayella beaten up, and he says Mayella claimed that Robinson had done it. Atticus draws from Tate an acknowledgment that it was Mayella's right side that was beaten. Mr. Ewell testifies that he heard Mayella screaming and that he found Robinson raping her. Ewell's uncouth language disturbs the courtroom. Atticus asks Ewell to write his name, and when Ewell does, it shows that Ewell is left-handed (and thus is likely to have been the one who beat up Mayella).

# Thought Questions (students consider while they read)

1. How is Jean Louise growing up and being socialized as a woman?
2. Why does Mr. Heck Tate knock on Atticus Finch's door (ch. 15)?
3. What does Atticus mean when he says, "a gang of wild animals *can* be stopped, simply because they're still human" (ch. 16)?
4. Why is it that "townsfolk rarely sat on juries, they were either struck or excused" (ch. 16)?

# Vocabulary (in order of appearance)

**Chapter 12**:

- habiliments: clothing
- haughty: condescending
- rotogravure: a printing process for images in newspapers
- denunciation: condemnation, severe criticism
- austere: serious and strict

## Chapter 13:

- shinny: alcohol, moonshine
- prerogative: privilege of having first choice
- tranquility: serenity, peace
- vetted: assessed and approved
- Reconstruction: the period just after the Civil War when the nation was recovering
- mandrake: a plant sometimes used for magic or fertility

## Chapter 14:

- penitentiary: jail
- manacles: handcuffs

## Chapter 15:

- venerable: highly respected
- aggregation: collection
- encumbered: weighed down

## Chapter 16:

- Mennonites: a nonviolent Protestant denomination similar to the Amish
- Prohibition: time period in the United States when alcohol was illegal (1920–1933)
- akimbo: bent outward
- Greek revival: a pre–Civil War architectural style reminiscent of ancient Greek buildings, which tended to be symmetrical and have white columns. Ancient Greece (because of Athens) was thought of as highly rational and democratic, features which were attractive to Americans in the first half of the 1800s.
- unobtrusive: inconspicuous, not in the way
- lanky: awkwardly tall and thin
- eccentricities: odd attributes

## Chapter 17:

- solicitor: lawyer
- gullet: throat
- corroborating evidence: support for an assertion or belief
- congenital: being present from birth
- acrimonious: in bitter conflict
- quelling: pacifying, suppressing
- immaterial: irrelevant

# Additional Homework

1. Tom Robinson's wife's name is Helen. Who was Helen of Troy? Write one or two sentences about Helen of Troy and then one sentence about why Harper Lee would give Tom Robinson's wife this symbolic name.

# Day 3 - Discussion of Thought Questions

1. How is Jean Louise growing up and being socialized as a woman?

**Time**: 10 minutes

**Discussion**: She sees that Jem is growing up. She doesn't want to act the way Jem thinks she should, but she appreciates Calpurnia's skill in the kitchen (ch. 12). She also sees Calpurnia stand up for what is right when she takes the children to her church. In chapter 13, Aunt Alexandra declares that she will help provide "some feminine influence." By the time, Jean Louise has learned the value of keeping silent at times and of lying "under certain circumstances"—are these strictly feminine conversation strategies in the novel, or do some of the male adults do the same thing? At the end of chapter 13, Jean Louise says, "I know now what he was trying to do, but Atticus was only a man. It takes a woman to do that kind of work." But in chapter 14, she is still resisting becoming a lady: "I felt the starched walls of a pink cotton penitentiary closing in on me."

2. Why does Mr. Heck Tate knock on Atticus Finch's door (ch. 15)?

**Time**: 5 minutes

**Discussion**: He has come with a group of men to warn Atticus about defending Tom Robinson. It is going to be a challenge to defend Tom in jail against the Ewell crowd, which might also attack Atticus. The men cannot understand why Atticus would take so much risk in defending Robinson. Jem thinks the group is a gang wanting to hurt Atticus, but Atticus says he has "never heard of a gang in Maycomb." This might be ironic, because the group is right and this statement will be wrong, since the predicted gang will come after Tom Robinson at the jail. But Atticus might realize that the gang will come after all, since he goes to wait for them overnight while Robinson is at the jail. In chapter 16 he will call them "a gang of wild animals."

3. What does Atticus mean when he says, "a gang of wild animals *can* be stopped, simply because they're still human" (ch. 16)?

**Time**: 5 minutes

**Discussion**: He is using a metaphor to suggest that the gang of people were acting like animals, being drunk and irrational and taking justice into their own hands. But humans are rational creatures who have conscience and other universal human traits. Even animalistic people are still human, because they can respond to the friendly conversation of a child and can feel empathy for others. Atticus says, "you children last night made Walter Cunningham stand in my shoes for a minute. That was enough." One minute of empathy gave Mr. Cunningham time to come to his senses.

4. Why is it that "townsfolk rarely sat on juries, they were either struck or excused" (ch. 16)?

**Time**: 5 minutes

**Discussion**: Atticus will give an answer in chapter 23: in the town, people have a lot of business connections. It would become awkward if they had to make decisions about justice against their business associates. But why is this reason unsatisfying? Is there a problem with standing up publicly for justice? Does business trump the law?

# Day 3 - Short Answer Quiz

1. Whose church do the children visit when Atticus is away?

_____

2. At the church, what is "linin'" or "lining"?

_____

3. Who most wants to give Jean Louise "some feminine influence"?

_____

4. Who engages Mr. Cunningham in conversation at the jail?

_____

5. What race of woman did Mr. Dolphus Raymond marry?

_____

6. According to Scout, what does her fight with Jem prove (ch. 14)?

_____

7. Is Robert Ewell left-handed or right-handed?

_____

8. What figure of speech is involved in the line, "The Governor was eager to scrape a few barnacles off the ship of state"?

_____

9. What is the most suspenseful thing about the novel so far?

_____

# Short Answer Quiz Key

1. Calpurnia's (or Reverend Sykes's, or the "black" church)
2. someone reads a line of a hymn and then everyone sings it
3. Aunt Alexandra (for discussion: does Atticus agree? Does Jem? Does Calpurnia?)
4. Jean Louise
5. black (for discussion: what race are his children? Why is this an important question for the people of Maycomb? Would this be an important question today?)
6. That they are equals
7. left-handed
8. metaphor (note: it is an extended metaphor, having multiple parts. Also: some alliteration.)
9. several possible answers (most likely: how the verdict will come out)

# Day 3 - Vocabulary Quiz

| Terms | Answers |
|---|---|

1. _____ acrimonious      A.  serious and strict
2. _____ solicitor         B.  highly respected
3. _____ haughty           C.  throat
4. _____ denunciation      D.  lawyer
5. _____ manacles          E.  being present from birth
6. _____ congenital        F.  condemnation, severe criticism
7. _____ austere           G.  weighed down
8. _____ venerable         H.  clothing
9. _____ eccentricities    I.  inconspicuous, not in the
10. _____ akimbo           J.  bent outward
11. _____ penitentiary     K.  condescending
12. _____ indigenous       L.  native, characteristic of a place
13. _____ aggregation      M.  jail
14. _____ immaterial       N.  pacifying, suppressing
15. _____ prerogative      O.  collection
16. _____ corroborating    P.  serenity, peace
17. _____ quelling         Q.  assessed and approved
18. _____ vetted           R.  in bitter conflict
19. _____ encumbered       S.  privilege of having first choice
20. _____ unobtrusive      T.  irrelevant
21. _____ habiliments      U.  odd attributes
22. _____ gullet           V.  supporting an assertion or belief
23. _____ tranquility      W.  handcuffs

# Vocabulary Quiz Answer Key

1. R
2. D
3. K
4. F
5. W
6. E
7. A
8. B
9. U
10. J
11. M
12. L
13. O
14. T
15. S
16. V
17. N
18. Q
19. G
20. I
21. H
22. C
23. P

# Day 3 - Classroom Activities

1. Dramatic reading

   **Kind of Activity**: Dramatic reading (large groups with whole class as audience). This activity differs from the "reading aloud" activity in that the students are in the roles of actors rather than simply being readers.
   **Objective**: Portray character through inflection and gesture, develop skill in enunciation, evoke a courtroom atmosphere
   **Time**: 10-15 minutes

   **Structure**:

   Students read part of chapter 17 aloud. The section should be read twice. Cast the loudest and more boisterous students first and the shy, quiet students last. Direct students to read only the dialogue and not the narrator's words. Assess the first performance before reading it a second time.

   The best section to read aloud consists of the first few pages from "in your own words, Mr. Tate" to "Which side again, Heck?" (speakers: Gilmer, Tate, Judge Taylor, Finch, and bit parts by court reporter, Scout, Jem).

   **Assessment Criteria**:

   1. Portraying character through inflection and gesture

   2. Enunciation

   3. Evocation of a courtroom atmosphere

2. What is socialization?

   **Kind of Activity**: small groups
   **Objective**: to experience the pressure of socialization and exclusion
   **Time**: about 15-20 minutes

   **Structure**:

   In this part of the book, we see how Scout is being socialized as a woman in her society. This exercise provides a sense of how easy it is to feel a strong pressure to socialize.

   Divide the class into groups of five. In each group, one person is the "unsocialized" person. A pile of jellybeans (about 20) is placed in the middle of each group. (Of course, if a student has dietary restrictions, an alternative food can be used.) The way to get to eat a jellybean is to praise something about another person in the group. First, the four "socialized" people take turns, for two rounds, praising one another and eating jellybeans. For the next two or three rounds until the jellybeans are gone, the "unsocialized" person takes turns as well.

Once the jellybeans are gone, the teacher instructs the groups to talk about the experience. The "unsocialized" students tell the others how it felt to be excluded without an opportunity to socialize and then later to be included, and the others talk about how it felt knowing that someone in the group was not able to fully participate, but then was included. Some students might talk about justice and fairness—simply not to have the opportunity seems unjust. Others might talk about pressure, wanting the "unsocialized" person to be able to participate. Others might say it is easy to get socialized into something when all you have to do is be nice and you get a reward, but what if you had to say something mean in order to get the reward? (The teacher can introduce these topics if no student brings them up.)

Finally, the teacher should ask students to imagine socialization pressure occurring all day every day for years. Those who fit in with the society tend to get the benefits, and those who do not will have to show special individual qualities in order to be appreciated and earn benefits. It becomes harder and harder to resist. Is this fair or unfair? What makes it so hard to appreciate uniqueness and individual differences? What about very basic patterns of socialization like personal grooming—or politeness, such as saying "please"?

**Assessment Criteria**:

* participation

* expression of one's experience

# Day 4 - Reading Assignment

Students read chapters 18-24.

## Daily Lesson Objectives

- Reading well: appreciating how the author is playing out each theme; appreciating how the author is weaving together the various threads of the narrative; enjoying the suspense of an emotionally charged trial.
- Thinking well: using the discussion questions and the trial to consider how to draw conclusions from evidence and to use evidence to weigh arguments and counterarguments.
- Speaking well: developing oral skills through vocabulary development, debate, and group discussion.
- Listening well: developing a taste for good grammar and strong diction by closely examining the testimony in the trial; evaluating oral arguments in the classroom activities.
- Writing well: creating and sustaining an argument, using evidence, in essay form.
- Understanding: seeing how themes of growing up, race, gender, class, and family are playing out in a specific town in Alabama.

Note that it is perfectly fine to expand any day's work into two days depending on the characteristics of the class, particularly if the class will engage in all of the suggested classroom exercises and activities and discuss all of the thought questions.

## Content Summary for Teachers

**Chapter 18**: Mayella is the next witness. She is very distraught. She testifies that Robinson raped her, she screamed, her father arrived, and Robinson ran away. Atticus cross-examines her and reveals her family's poverty. Mayella points out Robinson as the rapist. He stands and shows that his left arm is a foot shorter than his right arm—suggesting that he would not have used his left arm to beat Mayella on the right side. Mayella does poorly in the rest of the cross-examination.

**Chapter 19**: Robinson takes the stand. His left arm is so useless that he cannot use it at all. Atticus shows the jury how honest Robinson is. Robinson's testimony is completely different from the others'. He says he used to help her with chores, that Mayella was very lonely, and that she was the one who grabbed and kissed him. He resisted, but he ran away in fear once Mr. Ewell arrived. The prosecution's lawyer insults Robinson and expresses bitter racism. The proceedings make people of truly good morals feel sick.

**Chapter 20**: Mr. Dolphus Raymond, the town drunk, turns out to be faking it. Raymond explains that this pretense makes it easier for others to understand why he is so friendly toward black people in the town. Back in court, Atticus gives closing arguments and states that Mayella is the one who acted badly and broke the town's social code. Atticus brings the evidence together and suggests that Mr. Ewell beat his own daughter. Finally, it is the word of a black man against the word of several white people, racism versus justice. In a court of law, "all men are created equal," but a court is no more just than its jury.

**Chapter 21**: Calpurnia arrives in court with a note for Atticus: Aunt Alexandra cannot find the children. They are revealed and sent home for dinner but may return afterward. The courthouse is still packed when they return, everyone silent and still. The judge polls the jury, and every man declares Tom Robinson guilty. The black onlookers in the balcony rise to their feet to honor Atticus as he passes them on his way out of court.

**Chapter 22**: Jem is crying and angry and Atticus is exhausted; racism won out. The black community leaves Atticus all sorts of appreciative gifts. Jem is discouraged and disappointed with the people of Maycomb, but Miss Maudie points out that many white people helped on Robinson's side, including the sheriff and the judge. Miss Maudie sees a small advance against racism in this case. Mr. Ewell is seen at the post office threatening Atticus that he will "get him."

**Chapter 23**: Tom is being held on a prison farm, and his wife and children are not permitted to visit him. Jem and Atticus talk about juries; Jem no longer likes the idea. Women cannot serve on juries in Alabama, and many people want to stay out of the controversies because they have personal interests involved. In the specific case of Robinson, it was a Cunningham who held out for a verdict of innocence. Scout wants to invite Walter Cunningham for lunch, but Aunt Alexandra refuses because "he is trash." Jem is maybe getting chest hair and feels like a man, and he says that Alexandra is just trying to make Scout into a lady. Jem also reflects on social class in the county. Scout disagrees: "there's just one kind of folks. Folks." But Jem replies that people despise one another too much for that to be true.

**Chapter 24**: While Jem and Dill are out swimming, Aunt Alexandra has ladies over for a meeting of the Missionary Society of Maycomb, and Scout is there to learn to be a lady. The women discuss the plight of the Mruna people of Africa. A number of women make racist comments about their black helpers. Suddenly Atticus enters and privately reveals that Robinson tried to escape from prison and was shot to death by the prison guards. Atticus takes Calpurnia with him to tell Helen Robinson the news. Miss Maudie reflects on the good people of the town who respect Atticus and justice. Although Alexandra and Maudie are shaken, they join the other women effortlessly. Scout feels proud of her Aunt and Miss Maudie, and for the first time she feels inclined to be ladylike: "if Aunty could be a lady at a time like this, so could I."

Content Summary for Teachers

# Thought Questions (students consider while they read)

1. Why do Dill and Mr. Raymond feel sick at the end of chapter 19? What is Jem so upset about in chapter 23?
2. Why does Mr. Raymond portray himself as "badder'n you are already" (ch. 20)?
3. Do you agree with Atticus Finch's account of what happened between Tom and Mayella and why (ch. 20)? Does Tom's account make sense?
4. Why does Finch bring up Thomas Jefferson's line "that all men are created equal" (ch. 20)? In what ways are people equal or unequal?
5. Why does Miss Maudie say that Atticus is one of the people "in this world who were born to do our unpleasant jobs for us . . . We're so rarely called on to be Christians, but when we are, we've got men like Atticus to go for us" (ch. 22)?
6. How does Jean Louise learn to "be a lady" in chapter 24?

# Vocabulary (in order of appearance)

**Chapter 18**:

- strenuous: requiring great strength of effort
- chiffarobe: wardrobe or armoire including drawers
- brash: insensitive and tactless
- pilgrimage: a journey for a spiritual or noble reason

**Chapter 19**:

- ex cathedra: with absolute authority
- expunge: completely remove

**Chapter 20**:

- detachment: separation
- subsequent: next, following
- contraband: smuggled objects
- unmitigated: sustained, not moderated in intensity
- temerity: bold or reckless courage
- Rockefeller: American industrialist and oil monopolist around 1900

**Chapter 21**:

- foreman: leader of a jury or a work crew

**Chapter 22**:

- colleagues: coworkers, peers

**Chapter 23**:

- capital offense: crime deserving capital punishment (death)
- circumstantial: indirect
- wrathfully: with ire or anger
- inevitable: unavoidable

**Chapter 24**:

- charlotte: sponge cake from a cake mold, with filling
- impertinence: brazen disrespect
- squalor: great filthiness
- largo: slow speed
- undelectable: tasting bad

# Additional Homework

1. Read the opening paragraph of the Declaration of Independence. How are these principles relevant today? Jefferson thought they were universal, regardless of culture. Is there any place where it would be better to have a government based on the idea that there are no natural rights? Are human rights natural, inherent in each person, or does the government have to give people these rights? If rights are individual but people are diverse, why does American society generally value "equal rights"—is this because there are ways that every person is the same despite our differences? Write one to three paragraphs reflecting on one or more of these issues.

# Day 4 - Discussion of Thought Questions

1. Why do Dill and Mr. Raymond feel sick at the end of chapter 19? What is Jem so upset about in chapter 23?

**Time**: 5-10 minutes

**Discussion**:

Dill notes that Mr. Finch was respectful to Mayella Ewell and Mr. Ewell, while Mr. Gilmer was very disrespectful to Mr. Robinson. Mr. Gilmer called him "boy" and showed disgust when Mr. Robinson said he felt sorry for Mayella Ewell. Mr. Raymond does not explain why he feels sick, but it seems to be for similar reasons. It is clear that racism is making it very difficult for Mr. Robinson to get a fair trial. This goes far beyond the expectation that lawyers will be hard-hitting during cross-examinations.

Jem is upset that a jury would convict Mr. Robinson on such weak and exculpatory evidence. He is so upset he suggests doing away with juries. Atticus suggests that a better jury would have done the right thing, but the people who let prejudice get in the way of the facts are "trash."

We now see that the failure to rehabilitate Mr. Ewell actually is causing great costs to society after all. He has wrongly accused a man of beating and raping his daughter and has now involved the whole town as a result of his lie. This trial has cost many resources and has hurt the lives of the Finches as well as the Robinsons and Ewells, and it will lead to even more trouble.

2. Why does Mr. Raymond portray himself as "badder'n you are already" (ch. 20)?

**Time**: 5 minutes

**Discussion**: Since he cannot keep the racist townspeople from judging him for having married a black woman, he gives them an easy explanation for why he is of low character: he is a public drunkard. That leads people to generally leave him alone, which is what he wants. Is this a good strategy for being left alone to do what one likes?

3. Do you agree with Atticus Finch's account of what happened between Tom and Mayella and why (ch. 20)? Does Tom's account make sense?

**Time**: 5-10 minutes

**Discussion**: Tom and Atticus both have an interest in making the facts look like they point to Tom's innocence. But the evidence suggests that Tom could not have hit Mayella in a way that caused her physical injuries, so it makes sense to look for another explanation. If Mayella's father hit her, is this enough to say that Tom was innocent? The question becomes one of motive. Did Tom really have any motive to cheat on his wife, or is it more likely that Mayella really was so lonely that she had a motive to accost him?

4. Why does Finch bring up Thomas Jefferson's line "that all men are created equal" (ch. 20)? In what ways are people equal or unequal?

**Time**: 5-10 minutes

**Discussion**: Finch says that people are equal in every court of law; people are all equal before the law. This principle, along with Jefferson's in the Declaration of Independence, expresses something about our common humanity. According to Jefferson, people share the inalienable rights to life, liberty, and the pursuit of happiness simply because they are human beings. This basic equality does not mean that all people are the same in character. Some people are "stupid and idle," Atticus says, while others are "industrious." Even more, he says, some people are born with more potential and more opportunities. In the courts, everyone is innocent until proven guilty, but in many other areas of life, character and other kinds of merit matter. That is why teachers establish minimum passing grades for tests. People who do well enough can be promoted and move on, while those who fail should get another chance to learn what they did not learn. In Maycomb, some of the children pass out of first grade, but others fail and have to repeat it. Finch prefers that system to a system in which everyone gets to pass, which he calls "ridiculous."

5. Why does Miss Maudie say that Atticus is one of the people "in this world who were born to do our unpleasant jobs for us . . . We're so rarely called on to be Christians, but when we are, we've got men like Atticus to go for us" (ch. 22)?

**Time**: 5-10 minutes

**Discussion**: Miss Maudie understands that society has imperfections. Sometimes doing the right thing means going against society, and it is unpleasant to be in that position, because a society tends to sanction people who go against it. But a society tries to live up to certain principles like equality before the law, and even if many citizens do not want to give someone a fair trial, they support the idea of *someone* making sure that the system works. Even worse, in our representative government the people need representatives to serve in the legislature, but it is not very pleasant to be a legislator. Atticus is the kind of person who will serve his community and represent them, even if he does not like the opinions of most people he represents. Worst of all, being a Christian entails a high sense of justice, Miss Maudie implies, but again people send Atticus to do the right thing instead of doing it themselves.

6. How does Jean Louise learn to "be a lady" in chapter 24?

**Time**: 5-10 minutes

**Discussion**: She attends the meeting of the missionary circle and observes the habits and conversation of the women. She wears a dress (although her britches are still on, under the dress). She participates in the hospitality. She is a careful observer of how different women intervene in the conversation to redirect attention or to help people feel at ease (or to point a barb at someone politely). She reflects on hypocrisy and the ways that women can be hypocritical, comparing some of the faults of men she knows with the faults of women she knows. At the end of the chapter, she learns how to hide her sadness about Tom Robinson's death in order to rejoin the ladies in the group without revealing what she knows or how she feels. "After all," she reflects, "if Aunty could be a lady at a time like this, so could I."

# Day 4 - Short Answer Quiz

1. What is the name of Robert Ewell's oldest daughter?

_____

2. Is Thomas Robinson left-handed or right-handed?

_____

3. In what decade does the trial take place?

_____

4. Who walks into the courtroom with an envelope?

_____

5. Does the court find Robinson guilty or not guilty?

_____

6. When Mrs. Merriweather reports telling J. Grimes Everett that "the ladies of the Maycomb Alabama Methodist Episcopal Church South are behind you one hundred percent," Harper Lee is using what literary technique to communicate with the reader?

_____

7. What is really going on in the discussion among the women of Aunt Alexandra's missionary circle?

_____

8. What do you like or find most interesting about these chapters?

_____

# Short Answer Quiz Key

1. Mayella Violet Ewell
2. right-handed
3. the 1930s (the exact year is 1935)
4. Calpurnia
5. guilty
6. subtle satire to undercut someone
7. discussing racism; reinforcing social norms; practicing hospitality; providing that Scout is becoming grown up, etc.
8. many possible answers (some students will emphasize plot; others, character; others, themes—remember that questions like this one reinforce the idea that literature should be enjoyable as well as instructive)

# Day 4 - Vocabulary Quiz

## Terms

1. _____ brash
2. _____ capital offense
3. _____ charlotte
4. _____ chiffarobe
5. _____ circumstantial
6. _____ colleagues
7. _____ contraband
8. _____ detachment
9. _____ ex cathedra
10. _____ expunge
11. _____ foreman
12. _____ impertinence
13. _____ inevitable
14. _____ largo
15. _____ pilgrimage
16. _____ Rockefeller
17. _____ squalor
18. _____ strenuous
19. _____ subsequent
20. _____ temerity
21. _____ undelectable
22. _____ unmitigated
23. _____ wrathfully

## Answers

A. sponge cake from a mold, with filling
B. leader of a jury or a work crew
C. coworkers, peers
D. separation
E. American industrialist and oil monopolist
F. with absolute authority
G. a journey for a spiritual or noble reason
H. brazen disrespect
I. wardrobe or armoire including drawers
J. next, following
K. requiring great strength of effort
L. completely remove
M. slow speed
N. smuggled objects
O. indirect
P. great filthiness
Q. insensitive and tactless
R. unavoidable
S. bold or reckless courage
T. crime deserving death as punishment
U. tasting bad
V. with ire or anger
W. sustained, not moderated in intensity

# Vocabulary Quiz Answer Key

1. Q
2. T
3. A
4. I
5. O
6. C
7. N
8. D
9. F
10. L
11. B
12. H
13. R
14. M
15. G
16. E
17. P
18. K
19. J
20. S
21. U
22. W
23. V

# Day 4 - Classroom Activities

1. Courtroom debate

   **Kind of Activity**: argumentative debate
   **Objective**: Take a side and defend it, make oral arguments using evidence, assess oral arguments on the basis of evidence
   **Time**: 15-20 minutes

   **Structure**:

   The class splits into three groups for 5-8 minutes. One group, the defense, must develop the three best reasons why Tom Robinson is innocent. The other group, the prosecutors, must develop the three best reasons why he is guilty. The third group are the judges, who must try to anticipate what the other two groups will say. A spokesman for each of the two groups gives a two-minute presentation about the three reasons and the evidence for each reason.

   The judges take two or three minutes to determine which of the three reasons is strongest on each side, while each group decides which of the other group's reasons is the weakest. For the final five minutes, the judges explain which reasons are strongest and the two groups explain which reasons are weakest.

   **Assessment Criteria**:
   participation; effective use of evidence; speaking skills; critical thinking about arguments

2. Mock jury

   **Kind of Activity**: group discussion
   **Objective**: Take a side and defend it, make oral arguments using evidence, assess oral arguments on the basis of evidence
   **Time**: 15-20 minutes

   **Structure**:

   This is a more free-flowing version of the first activity. The class splits into groups of 12 to simulate juries. Half of each group is assigned to emphasize why Tom Robinson might be innocent, and the other half is assigned to emphasize why Tom Robinson might be guilty. The jurors are told that at the end, they will vote openly on whether he is "innocent" or "guilty" and silently (using a piece of paper) on who made the best argument and deserves to be the "foreman" of the jury.

After 5-8 minutes, all jurors are freed from this constraint to assess all the evidence freely.

Each jury member then writes his or her vote for foreman on a piece of paper. The votes are tallied (for the sake of time, ties will be broken by declaration of the teacher). The foreman then calls for jurors to raise their hands for "guilty" and then for "innocent."

The juries then reassemble and report their results.

It may well be that all juries unanimously find Robinson innocent, for the author has made him seem innocent and has strongly implied that one must be a racist in order to see Robinson as guilty.

Discussion then follows: what is it that made Robinson's jury in the book unanimously find him guilty, while the juries today (presumably) found him innocent? Is racism the only reason he was found guilty?

**Assessment Criteria**:
participation; effective use of evidence; speaking skills; critical thinking about arguments

# Day 5 - Reading Assignment

Students read chapters 25-31.

## Daily Lesson Objectives

- Reading well: appreciating the achievement of the author by examining how each theme culminates and interlocks with other themes, and how the author combines tone, feelings, suspense, arguments, and humor to carry the reader's interest; carefully examining the details of the altercation in order to learn how to find clues about plot developments.
- Thinking well: using the discussion questions to draw conclusions from evidence and to consider how rational people make difficult moral decisions that involve justice, the law, and the sense of common decency; assessing the likelihood of alternative depictions of an event
- Speaking well: developing oral skills through vocabulary development, debate, individual presentation, dramatic reenactment, and group discussion.
- Listening well: developing a taste for good grammar and strong diction; evaluating oral arguments and dramatic presentations.
- Writing well: creating and sustaining a descriptive essay, using evidence, in essay form.
- Understanding: seeing how themes of justice, growing up, race, gender, class, and family matter to different people in different ways.

Note that it is perfectly fine to expand any day's work into two days depending on the characteristics of the class, particularly if the class will engage in all of the suggested classroom exercises and activities and discuss all of the thought questions.

## Content Summary for Teachers

**Chapter 25**: It is September. Jem stops Scout from killing an insect—they are growing mature. Robsinon's death was taken as a "typical" matter of course in Maycomb, and Scout reflects that given "the secret courts of men's hearts," Atticus could have said nothing to get Robinson declared innocent. Upon hearing that Robinson died, Mr. Ewell is rumored to have said, "one down and about two more to go," but this threat is unclear.

**Chapter 26**: School has started. Scout no longer fears the Radley house. Scout's and Jem's classmates are cold, seemingly because of Atticus's defense of Robinson. One day in class, the teacher compares Nazi Germany unfavorably to America, where "we don't believe in persecuting anybody," but Scout sees Miss Gates as extremely hypocritical because of the racism expressed during Robinson's trial. Scout brings this up with Jem, but Jem responds in anger, wanting to forget all about the Robinson situation.

**Chapter 27**: Mr. Ewell seems to be preparing his revenge: Judge Taylor sees a prowler, and Mr. Ewell trails Helen Robinson to work. For Halloween, Grace Merriweather writes a pageant for the people of Maycomb about their county's history. The children are to play the parts of Maycomb's agricultural products, and Scout has the part of the pork. Her costume is made of chicken wire covered with brown cloth and is hard for Scout to see through. Jem escorts her as the pork to the pageant without Atticus or Aunt Alexandra.

**Chapter 28**: Jem and Scout walk to the school for the pageant and country fair, and it is very dark. Cecil Jacobs and Scout entertain themselves at the fair. At the pageant, Scout falls asleep waiting for the very long segment on the history of Maycomb to end. She awakens during the last song and realizes she has missed her cue. She rushes onstage and makes a hilarious entrance. She feels embarrassed and waits backstage with Jem until everyone leaves. She finally leaves for home with Jem, still wearing the costume. They hear a strange noise, then footsteps, then someone running after them. There is a struggle that ends with a man on the ground (he is dead) and another man carrying Jem home unconscious with a broken arm. At home the sheriff is called. The man outside is Mr. Ewell, dead with a kitchen knife in his ribs.

**Chapter 29**: Scout tells what she thinks happened. Sheriff Tate notes the knife mark on Scout's costume as evidence of intent to harm. Scout looks at the man who carried Jem and realizes he is Boo Radley. She says, "Hey, Boo."

**Chapter 30**: Trying to be as friendly as possible, Scout leads Boo to the back porch, where everyone is gathering. The others are discussing who killed Mr. Ewell. Atticus thinks that Jem must have done it since Scout named Jem as her protector in her story, but the sheriff insists that Mr. Ewell fell onto his knife and killed himself. The discussion disturbs Atticus, who stands for truth and justice without exceptions. After much arguing, the sheriff finally yells that he is trying to protect Boo, not Jem, and urges Atticus to keep Boo out of the limelight even if it means bending the truth. Atticus, deeply moved by the revelation that Boo saved his children, asks Scout if she understands why they are agreeing to protect Boo. Scout says yes, because to involve Boo would be like shooting a mockingbird. Atticus looks at Scout with a sense of wonder, and he thanks Boo.

**Chapter 31**: Boo wants to touch Jem, so Scout helps him by showing him how to gently stroke Jem's hair. She helps him home, allowing him to escort her down the block, just like a lady should. The narrator, speaking as an older Scout, says she never saw him again. Standing on Boo's porch, Scout looks out over the neighborhood imagining how Boo must have seen it and watched over the children. Back home, Scout falls asleep while Atticus reads to her, and she wakes up while he carries her to bed. She says that the book he read was about a character who was chased and caught but then found to be innocent and "real nice." Atticus replies, "most people are, when you finally see them." Atticus spends the rest of the night by Jem's side.

# Thought Questions (students consider while they read)

1. Why does Jem discourage Scout from killing the roly-poly? (ch. 25).
2. What are the clues about who killed Mr. Ewell (ch. 28)?
3. When Mr. Tate and Mr. Finch are maneuvering in chapter 30, what is really going on?
4. Why does Scout say to Mr. Arthur, "bend your arm down here, like that" (ch. 31)?

# Vocabulary (in order of appearance)

### Chapter 25:

- assurances: promises designed to alleviate concerns

### Chapter 26:

- prosecuting: bringing charges against
- persecuting: treating badly, often because of one's characteristics

### Chapter 27:

- nondescript: plain, unremarkable

### Chapter 28:

- mortification: strong embarrassment
- scuffling: fighting
- staccato: a punctuated rhythm of short separated bursts
- untrammeled: unrestrained, free

### Chapter 29:

- perforated: having one or more holes punched through
- garish: gaudy, embarrassingly showy
- indentations: spaces, cuts, dents

### Chapter 30:

- blandly: unremarkably boring or without flavor
- blunt: direct and without apology, broad and not sharp

### Chapter 31:

- glistened: shined
- sedative: substance used to induce sleep
- scampered: scurried
- amiable: friendly
- acquiescence: capitulation, easy consent
- shrewder: more cunning and pragmatic

# Additional Homework

1. Finding Your Local History

   Grace Merriweather writes a pageant for the people of Maycomb about their county's history. Do you know the highlights of the history of your city or your county? Learn a few things about your local history, choosing your city or your county. Do this research by going to the library, a local museum, or a local landmark, or by asking someone who has lived in the area for at least 25 years. Do not simply use the Internet.

   (Teachers can provide a list of local landmarks for students to visit. This assignment might be given a few days ahead of time so that students have a chance to visit some sites during business hours.)

   In an essay of about five or six paragraphs, tell the story of what you did to learn this history and what you found out.

# Day 5 - Discussion of Thought Questions

1. Why does Jem discourage Scout from killing the roly-poly? (ch. 25).

**Time**: 2-3 minutes

**Discussion**: Jem's new charity for even the world of insects reflects his new appreciation for life in all its forms. It also symbolizes the principle of human justice that revolves around the idea of not hurting someone if "they don't bother you."

2. What are the clues about who killed Mr. Ewell (ch. 28)?

**Time**: 10 minutes

**Discussion**:

Close reading of the text is essential here. Remember also that Scout is recalling the events, and then she is recalling her conversation in chapter 29, and her recollections may not be accurate in either case.

Jem and Scout had yelled, so there was opportunity for someone nearby to hear the shouting and join the group. When Scout first goes down, she hears "scuffling, kicking sounds, sounds of shoes and flesh"—is someone already helping them? Probably not, since the attacker still has the upper hand: Jem's arm is broken soon afterward (we will learn), and Scout's arms are pinned. But then someone must be strong enough for Ewell to be "jerked backwards and flung on the ground"—this is where someone probably came to help. Jem's arm is broken, so he probably cannot be the one who did it. Mr. Ewell probably is the one who coughs violently as he dies, so the "man's heavy breathing" probably is the defender's. This is the same person who drags something heavy (we soon learn that it is Jem) over the ground and toward the road. (That person turns out to be Mr. Radley.)

At the end of chapter 28, we learn that Mr. Ewell died with "a kitchen knife stuck up under his ribs." We do not know if it was Mr. Ewell's knife or someone else's. It seems to be Mr. Ewell's, since it seems that a knife was used to make "a shiny clean line" on Scout's costume (ch. 29). Still, Jem might not be tall enough yet to get a good knife shot into Mr. Ewell's ribs, which again points to Mr. Radley.

3. When Mr. Tate and Mr. Finch are maneuvering in chapter 30, what is really going on?

**Time**: 10-15 minutes

**Discussion**:

Again close reading is essential. Mr. Finch suggests that Jem killed Mr. Ewell in self defense. On the basis of Scout's report this scenario is possible, and Mr. Finch says "there's no doubt about it." But in an earlier chapter he said that one should not convict if there is even a shadow of a doubt, and Mr. Finch has plenty of reason to doubt, since Mr. Radley was on the scene, and in light of the previous thought question. Why would he insist on Jem being the killer when Boo Radley could have done it (and probably did it)? He seems to be insisting in order to protect Boo Radley.

When Mr. Tate says, "hold on. Jem never stabbed Bob Ewell," Mr. Tate wants to pin the death on Mr. Ewell himself, falling on his own knife. This would protect both Jem and Boo. Mr. Finch sees that implication clearly and says that it is very kind of Mr. Tate to protect Jem, but it would be immoral to 'hush up' or manipulate the reporting of the events. If so, then why would he be protecting Boo? Is it possible that Mr. Finch really is sure that Jem did it? Mr. Finch's morals are very strong, and he understands that it is better to submit oneself for justice than to try to evade justice; he tells Mr. Tate that the best way to serve his son is to confront reality honestly together with Jem, not to hush up the events.

Heck Tate insists that he can prove that Mr. Ewell fell on his knife, but Atticus still says "I won't have it." When Tate shouts back, *"God damn it, I'm not thinking of Jem!"* is he thinking of Boo Radley, or does he honestly think Ewell fell on his knife? Is he thinking of what would happen to Jem's family if Jem were accused?

Atticus realizes that the switchblade might have been Ewell's (Tate admits he "took it off a drunk man"), which would mean that the kitchen knife probably came from Boo Radley. Tate says, however, that Ewell probably had the kitchen knife to begin with. Tate again says that it is his own responsibility to report the events however he wants, pulling rank as the county sheriff. His argument is that Ewell was the cause of Robinson's death, so it is fair that "the dead bury the dead."

Finally Tate admits that he is talking about Arthur Radley, at the end of the chapter, without mentioning his name. He suggests Radley is a "citizen" who did "his utmost to prevent a crime from being committed." The effect of having it known that Radley saved the children would be "draggin' him with his shy ways into the limelight—to me, that's a sin. ... If it was any other man it'd be different." If it is a sin to kill a mockingbird, it is also a sin to drag a shy person into the public eye when he just wanted to do a good deed.

Atticus considers this "for a long time" before asking Scout to understand that she should go along with the lie that Mr. Ewell fell on his knife. Scout wants to reassure him, so she says she understands, but she agrees also because she understands why the lie might be valuable. She points out that bringing Boo Radley back into the public eye after a killing would be "sort of like shootin' a mockingbird."

4. Why does Scout say to Mr. Arthur, "bend your arm down here, like that" (ch. 31)?

**Time**: 2-5 minutes

**Discussion**: Having one's arm bent is a symbol of bending to society's norms. In this case, it also is literally what Radley needs to do to show that he is a gentleman, as though he were the one escorting Scout (not the reverse). Scout creates this lie and this scenario in order to forestall gossip from someone like Stephanie Crawford. She has become wise to the ways that an adult woman can perceive a situation and put on the proper appearances to make everyone feel at ease.

# Day 5 - Short Answer Quiz

1. Who likens Tom Robinson's death to "the senseless slaughter of songbirds"?

   _____

2. In class, Miss Gates writes on the blackboard, "WE ARE A _____"

   _____

3. What kind of government does Miss Gates say that Germany has?

   _____

4. Who notices the hypocrisy of people who hate Hitler's racism but do not mind the racism of the people in Maycomb?

   _____

5. In the pageant, what is Jean Louise supposed to be?

   _____

6. Although it is not intended to be, does the pageant end up as a comedy, romance, or tragedy?

   _____

7. With what weapon is Mr. Ewell killed?

_____

8. Which of the following plot elements is NOT present in this section of the book? (a) introduction (b) rising action (c) climax (d) falling action (e) denouement

_____

9. Who suffers poetic justice for the death of Tom Robinson?

_____

10. When Scout thinks that there is not much else left to learn, "except possibly algebra," it is an example of the author using which device? (a) sarcasm (b) irony (c) mathematical analogy (d) symbolism

_____

11. At the end of the novel, who does Stoner's Boy symbolize?

_____

12. Describe Mr. Arthur (Boo) Radley with two adjectives that you might not have used about him until the final chapters.

_____

# Short Answer Quiz Key

1. Mr. Underwood (in his editorial)
2. DEMOCRACY
3. a dictatorship
4. Jean Louise
5. pork/ham
6. comedy
7. a kitchen knife
8. (a) introduction
9. Robert Ewell
10. (b) irony
11. Arthur (Boo) Radley
12. many possible answers, such as "courageous," "respectful," "nervous," or "sweet"

# Day 5 - Vocabulary Quiz

## Terms

1. _____ acquiescence
2. _____ amiable
3. _____ assurances
4. _____ blandly
5. _____ blunt
6. _____ garish
7. _____ glistened
8. _____ indentations
9. _____ mortification
10. _____ nondescript
11. _____ perforated
12. _____ persecuting
13. _____ prosecuting
14. _____ scampered
15. _____ scuffle
16. _____ sedative
17. _____ shrewder
18. _____ staccato
19. _____ untrammeled

## Answers

A. bringing charges against
B. shined
C. unrestrained, free
D. capitulation, easy consent
E. substance used to induce sleep
F. direct and without apology, broad and not sharp
G. unremarkably boring or without flavor
H. promises designed to alleviate concerns
I. strong embarrassment
J. fight
K. spaces, cuts, dents
L. friendly
M. a punctuated rhythm of short separated bursts
N. scurried
O. plain, unremarkable
P. treating badly, often because of one's characteristics
Q. having one or more holes punched through
R. more cunning and pragmatic
S. gaudy, embarrassingly showy

# Vocabulary Quiz Answer Key

1. D
2. L
3. H
4. G
5. F
6. S
7. B
8. K
9. I
10. O
11. Q
12. P
13. A
14. N
15. J
16. E
17. R
18. M
19. C

# Day 5 - Classroom Activities

1. What really happened that night?

    **Kind of Activity**: dramatic reenactment
    **Objective**: Use imagination to reenact a scene, take a side and defend it, make oral arguments using evidence, assess possibilities on the basis of evidence
    **Time**: 20 minutes

    **Structure**:

    This activity should occur *after* discussion of the third thought question. The class splits into four groups for 10 minutes. Three of the groups will have 4 people, with one person playing each role of Jem, Scout, Mr. Ewell, and Boo Radley. Each of these three groups spends the 10 minutes preparing a brief, 2-minute skit to reenact what happened when Jem and Scout were attacked. In one group, Mr. Ewell falls on his own knife. In another group, Jem kills Mr. Ewell with a knife. In the third group, Boo kills Mr. Ewell with a knife.

    The fourth group consists of the judges. (There might be several groups of judges depending on class size, with each group of judges consisting of about 4 students.) This group spends the 10 minutes deciding which elements should be in the skit (the broken arm, the slashing of the costume, etc.), and advanced groups could spend time considering which facts are most important for judging what really happened (for example, when does Jem's arm get broken, how many weapons are really on the scene, and at what point does Boo Radley arrive?).

    The three groups perform their skits, and then the judges discuss what they saw and whether the stories, as reenacted, are believable.

    **Assessment Criteria**:
    participation; accurate use of evidence from the text; speaking and performance skills; critical thinking about arguments

2. Oral Presentation on Local History

    **Kind of Activity**: oral presentations
    **Objective**: Develop speaking skills, share in a common history, understand linkages between literature and history and that every place has a history
    **Time**: 10-30 minutes

**Structure**: selected students give informal presentations about their papers on local history—on both their methods of gaining information and the information itself. Ask other students to fill in the details if their own papers include details that have not been mentioned. If students have conflicting details, ask them to consider how they might figure out what really happened. Make sure to add key elements of local history if no student mentions them, and help students put certain details in context if necessary (for example, different periods of history; political, social, or economic conditions; the common moral norms of other generations). Consider asking what it would be like if the town put on a pageant of its history.

**Assessment Criteria**:
participation; oral presentation skills (projection, clarity, and so on).

# Final Paper

## Essay Questions

1. How does Scout learn that "You never really understand a person ... until you climb into his skin and walk around in it" (ch. 3)?

2. How is it that Atticus "is the same in his house as he is on the public streets" (ch. 5)?

3. How are Jem and Scout learning about themselves and their society? How is Jean Louise being socialized as a woman?

4. What is Boo Radley all about?

5. Why is Atticus Finch defending Tom Robinson?

6. What makes Dill and Mr. Raymond feel sick at the end of chapter 19, and what makes Jem so upset in chapter 23?

7. Does *To Kill a Mockingbird* exhibit a respect for life?

## Advice on research sources

A. School or community library

Ask your reference librarian for help locating books on the following subjects:

* Harper Lee and her literary generation

* To Kill a Mockingbird

* The Depression

* The American South

* Racism

* Growing Up

B. Personal interviews

* Ask people who were young before 1965 about their experience of the civil rights movement in America.

* Ask people who are from small towns what life was like when they were children.

C. Personal experience

Have you ever thought it would be better to lie in order to make someone feel at ease? Have you ever thought you should lie for an even more important reason? Have you experienced racism? What has it been like for you to be socialized as a man or a woman?

# Grading rubric for essays

Style:

* words: spelling and diction

* sentences: grammar and punctuation

* paragraphs: organization

* essay: structure

* argument: rhetoric, reasonableness, creativity

Content:

* accuracy

* use of evidence

* addresses the question

* completeness

* uses literary concepts

# Final Paper Answer Key

Remember that essays about literature should not be graded with a cookie-cutter approach whereby specific words or ideas are required. See the grading rubric above for a variety of criteria to use in assessing answers to the essay questions. This answer key thus functions as a store of ideas for students who need additional guidance in framing their answers.

1. How does Scout learn that "You never really understand a person ... until you climb into his skin and walk around in it" (ch. 3)?

   Understanding someone often means seeing the world from his or her point of view. A good structure for answering this question involves Scout's perceptions of different characters. Through her experiences, she comes to learn what each person values, feels, and believes. She sees her father's sense of justice; she feels the sting of racism when she experiences it herself at Calpurnia's church; she imagines what Boo Radley is like but does not really understand him until the end; she resists traditional femininity but finally starts to understand its positive role in her society at the end, when she sees the value of helping visitors feel secure and comfortable in one's home.

   An alternative structure for answering this question involves a deep look at Scout's experience of one particular character. An outstanding essay might point out the ways that she sees complexity in a character, such as when she internalizes the difficulty her father feels in letting Boo Radley off the hook in the matter of Mr. Ewell's murder. Understanding a person means understanding the person's inner conflicts as well as the person's thoughts and feelings.

2. How is it that Atticus "is the same in his house as he is on the public streets" (ch. 5)?

   According to Miss Maudie, Atticus does not show hypocrisy. He is the same in private as he is in public. Whatever principles of honor and conduct he talks about on the street, he tries to live out at home. A good answer to this question will examine how Atticus expresses these principles. Situations one might expect to find include Atticus's choice to defend Tom, his decision to guard the jail, his punishment of Jem for cutting off the tops of Mrs. Dubose's camellia (flower) bushes, and his decision to accept the sheriff's account of events at the end. Each of these situations shows a fairly consistent sense of justice—even if, in the last instance, justice means acquiescing to the sheriff instead of following the letter of the law.

An outstanding essay might point out that the high morality that Scout sees, as narrator, might be far less than objective. After all, Scout is remembering her father very fondly as a great man, but isn't that what a lot of children do, even against the truth?

3. How are Jem and Scout learning about themselves and their society? How is Jean Louise being socialized as a woman?

The children are in school, but they are learning a great deal outside of school from their father and Calpurnia as well as from observing one another and others in the town. A good answer to this question will focus on a number of specific events when someone learns a lesson, with one example in each mode: learning in school, learning from other adults, and learning from experience.

Scout learns to be a woman both by watching other women and by being told what to do. She appreciates some things that women in her society are good at, such as Calpurnia's skill in the kitchen. Her Aunt Alexandra specifically works to provide "some feminine influence" for Jean Louise. The key scene is the women's missionary circle at the end. A good essay might contrast her childish ways with her more womanly ways, particularly focusing on the beginning and end of the novel. Another good essay might contrast what women do and what men do in the novel, considering how much of each pattern rubs off on Scout. In addition, an essay might confront Scout's resistance and independence.

4. What is Boo Radley all about?

A good structure for this topic is to begin with the children's fears about Boo Radley, then to track the various episodes that show his compassion. He probably folded up Jem's pants after he lost them at Boo's house. He probably is the one who gave the children gifts in the tree. He also probably put a blanket on Jean Louise during the fire at Miss Maudie's house. But is he also the person who killed a man in defense of the children? If he is so compassionate, the essay should address why he has been locked up in the house (such as the possibility that he is easily prone to violence when angered).

An outstanding essay might infer additional characteristics about Boo Radley by examining what others (especially the adults) say about him and how they act towards him. For instance, why would Atticus be so interested in considering Boo as symbolically a mockingbird?

5. Why is Atticus Finch defending Tom Robinson?

Even if this topic has been discussed in detail in class, it is a good exercise for students to get this topic organized on paper. A good essay will go through the "number of reasons" that Finch has for defending Robinson: respect for the law, a chance to teach the community (and his children) about racism and justice, and his personal moral code or conscience. These reasons are tied to together in Finch's desire to do what is right even if others disagree. A good essay will examine such topics by providing evidence for these character traits. An outstanding essay might also include the pressures on Finch not to defend Robinson, including the racism of his society, the treatment of him and his children, and even the risk to his life on the night when he guards Robinson's cell.

6. What makes Dill and Mr. Raymond feel sick at the end of chapter 19, and what makes Jem so upset in chapter 23?

Dill notes that Mr. Finch was respectful to Mayella Ewell and Mr. Ewell, while Mr. Gilmer was very disrespectful to Mr. Robinson. Mr. Gilmer called him "boy" and showed disgust when Mr. Robinson said he felt sorry for Mayella Ewell. Mr. Raymond likewise seems to feel sick because racism is making it very difficult for Mr. Robinson to get a fair trial. Jem is upset that a jury would convict Mr. Robinson on such weak and exculpatory evidence. The key to this essay is to recognize the feeling of disgust that these three share. Each one's conscience is disturbed by the racist treatment of Mr. Robinson. An outstanding essay might point out that "racism" alone is not what makes them feel so sick; it is seeing racism in action against a specific individual, intensified by seeing the hypocrisy of people in a town that they feel ties to.

7. Does *To Kill a Mockingbird* exhibit a respect for life?

Key points for this essay might include these: (1) The citizens who respect life wish Mr. Robinson were alive, and the worst citizens want him dead and might be going to the jail to do it themselves. (2) Mockingbirds cannot be shot, but blue jays and rabid dogs can be shot. Does this mean that only useful or friendly life is respected? (3) A person can kill another in order to save someone else's life.

In light of these points, the novel seems to demonstrate respect for innocent life but violent justice for those who are guilty. But if that is the case, the town has not yet met the justice it deserves for treating Mr. Robinson so badly. The point here is that even if the town does not respect life very well, the novel sides with Atticus, who does respect life.

# Final Exam

## A. Multiple Choice

Circle the letter corresponding to the best answer.

1. What makes Scout unusual as a student in the first grade?

    (A) She is taller than all the others
    (B) She can outrun all the boys
    (C) She speaks a foreign language
    (D) She can read and write

2. How much time do the Ewell children normally spend in school?

    (A) None at all
    (B) On and off until about the sixth grade
    (C) Most of the time, except during harvest season
    (D) Only the first day of each year

3. Why does Mr. Radley shoot at Jem, Dill and Scout?

    (A) He catches them stealing money hidden in a tree in his yard
    (B) He catches them reenacting the time when Boo Radley stabbed his father
    (C) Jem accidentally shoots the Radley house with his gun
    (D) They are in the Radley yard trying to peek into a window

4. When Mr. Radley plugs the knot-hole in the tree, what does his action best symbolize or suggest?

    (A) The loss of childhood pleasures and the transition to adulthood responsibilities
    (B) The futile attempt to prolong life by patching up deadly wounds
    (C) The negative effects of generosity
    (D) The limitations on Boo Radley's interactions with others

5. What is the main reason why Atticus accepts a case that he knows he will lose?

    (A) He is friends with the Robinson family
    (B) To maintain his conscience and integrity
    (C) To raise a furor in the town of Maycomb
    (D) He needs the money

6. What is suggested by the killing of the rabid dog by Atticus?

(A) The end of his time as a single father
(B) His desire to put down the mob that wants to lynch Tom Robinson
(C) His desire to end conflicts swiftly by using force
(D) His inability to defend those who are guilty

7. Which character is metaphorically compared with a mockingbird at the end of the novel?

(A) Tom Robinson
(B) Boo Radley
(C) Atticus Finch
(D) Scout Finch

8. What is the main reason Mrs. Dubose has Jem read to her every day for over a month?

(A) She is dying and cannot read for herself anymore
(B) She is bored and wants the company
(C) She wants to punish Jem by making him do something he hates
(D) She is a morphine addict and is using the time to wean herself off the drug

9. When Calpurnia takes Jem and Scout to her church, what is different about her?

(A) She speaks with a black dialect
(B) She is distracted by the fact that Atticus is away from town
(C) She ignores them in favor of other children
(D) She argues that morality is a sham

10. What happens at the church when Calpurnia brings the Finch children?

(A) Everyone claps vigorously for the visitors
(B) The Reverend asks her to leave
(C) The children misbehave
(D) The children meet with a brief objection, but overall they are welcomed

11. Which crucial piece of evidence leads us to believe that Tom Robinson did not hit and rape Mayella?

(A) Tom's left arm is useless, making it nearly impossible for him to have caused her injuries
(B) Tom frequently stopped by the Ewell residence, so his story is believable
(C) Mayella hesitates before answering questions, suggesting that she is lying
(D) Mr. Ewell is a drunkard, so he probably hit her himself

12. What happens to Tom after his conviction?

(A) He is put to death by hanging
(B) He is freed and reunited with his family
(C) He is exiled from the county
(D) He is shot while trying to escape

13. By reporting that Bob Ewell fell onto his own knife, whom does the sheriff protect?

(A) Jem Finch
(B) Boo Radley
(C) Atticus Finch
(D) Scout Finch

14. Why is Scout late for her entrance at the pageant?

(A) She was spying on Boo Radley
(B) She was fighting with Walter Cunningham backstage
(C) She fell asleep
(D) She couldn't get her costume on

15. At the end of the novel, where is Atticus?

(A) At Jem's bedside
(B) Surveying the neighborhood from the front porch
(C) Comforting Scout in the living room
(D) In the study reading a book

# B. Short Answer

1. Who is described by the following sentence? "All the little man on the witness stand had that made him any better than his nearest neighbors was, that if scrubbed with lye soap in very hot water, his skin was white."

   ─────────────────────────────────────

2. Who says, "There was no doubt about it, I must soon enter this world, where on its surface fragrant ladies rocked slowly, fanned gently, and drank cool water"?

   ─────────────────────────────────────

3. Use three adjectives to describe each of the following characters. Choose adjectives that make each character seem as unique as possible (not "male" or "young"), without stretching the truth.

   A. Jem

   B. Scout

   C. Atticus

   D. Alexandra

   E. Boo Radley

   ─────────────────────────────────────

# C. Vocabulary

## Terms    Answers

1. _____ aberrations A. added attributesbr/B. acknowledgments in favor of the other side in an
2. _____ acquiescence argument/C. serious and strictbr/D. confusionbr/E. sustained, not
3. _____ auspicious moderated in intensitybr/F. treating badly, often because of one's
4. _____ austere characteristicsbr/G. slight disorders or
5. _____ benevolent problems/H. unavoidablebr/I. suggesting good
6. _____ concessions luck/J. goodwillbr/K. deserted,
7. _____ desolate ruined/L. gentlemanlybr/M. condescendingbr/N. sincerebr/O. trouble
8. _____ eccentricities situations/P. characterized by being localbr/Q. bringing charges
9. _____ gallant against/R. serenity, peacebr/S. irrelevantbr/T. capitulation, easy conse
10. _____ haughty
11. _____ immaterial
12. _____ indigenous
13. _____ inevitable
14. _____ ingenuous
15. _____ perplexity
16. _____ persecuting
17. _____ prosecuting
18. _____ tranquility
19. _____ unmitigated
20. _____ vexations

# D. Short Essays

1. Describe in your own words what happened between Mayella Ewell and Tom Robinson.

_____

_____

_____

_____

2. What are the clues about who killed Mr. Ewell, and what do the clues suggest?

_____

_____

_____

_____

3. When Mr. Tate and Mr. Finch are maneuvering to determine how to describe what happened during Mr. Ewell's attack on Scout and Jem, what is really going on?

_____

_____

_____

_____

D. Short Essays

# Final Exam Answer Key

## A. Multiple Choice Answer Key

1. D
2. D
3. D
4. D
5. B
6. B
7. B
8. D
9. A
10. D
11. A
12. D
13. B
14. C
15. A

## B. Short Answer Key

1. Mr. Robert Ewell
2. Jean Louise Finch
3. There are many possible answers. The point is not to be right or wrong, hopefully, but to be more or less precise. Teachers will know whether most adjectives chosen by students are relevant and true. Students may be encouraged later on to defend the adjec

## C. Vocabulary Answer Key

1. G
2. T
3. I
4. C

5. J
6. B
7. K
8. A
9. L
10. M
11. S
12. P
13. H
14. N
15. D
16. F
17. Q
18. R
19. E
20. O

# D. Short Essays Answer Key

1. In general: she invited him to help as she had done often in the past, she got him to come in to help, she went after him to gratify herself, he resisted and tried to leave, and they were seen by Mr. Ewell. Robinson did not hit her but ran away.

2. Since Jem and Scout yelled, someone nearby probably heard them. Someone is strong enough for Ewell to be "jerked backwards and flung on the ground." The "man's heavy breathing" that Scout hears probably is the person who killed Ewell. This is the same person who then drags Jem over the ground and toward the road. That person turns out to be Mr. Radley. When we learn that Mr. Ewell died with "a kitchen knife stuck up under his ribs," this point also suggests that Boo Radley was the defender.

3. Atticus suggests that Jem killed Mr. Ewell in self defense. Mr. Tate wants to pin the death on Mr. Ewell himself, which would protect both Jem and Boo. Finch does not want to lie about what happened, though. Tate pulls rank as the sheriff and persuades Atticus that this is the best way to serve justice since Radley needs to be protected, and Ewell got what he deserved. Finch finally agrees that bringing Boo Radley back into the public eye after a killing would be unjust, "sort of like shootin' a mockingbird."

# Lesson Plans

*Getting you the grade since 1999*™

## Other Lesson Plans from GradeSaver™

To Kill a Mockingbird

Made in the USA
Lexington, KY
23 April 2013